The Kingdom of the Subjunctive

The
Kingdom
of the
Subjunctive

Poems by Suzanne Wise

Alice James Books
FARMINGTON, MAINE

Library of Congress Cataloging-in-Publication Data

Wise, Suzanne. 1965-

The kingdom of the subjunctive : poems / by Suzanne Wise.

p. cm.

ISBN 1-882295-23-4 (alk. paper)

1. Feminism Poetry. 2. Women Poetry. I. Title.

PS3573.I7985K56 2000

811'.54—dc21

Grateful acknowledgment is made to the editors of the following magazines in which these poems first appeared: *Bellingham Review:* "Autobiography," *Boston Review:* "Highway to English," *Columbia Poetry Review:* "Maneuvers," *Denver Quarterly:* "Lunchtime in the Kingdom of the Subjunctive," *Fence:* "Advice," *Lit:* "Nicht," *Pierogi Press:* "More Advice," *Provincetown Arts:* "Wise Comma Suzanne," *Quarter After Eight:* "50 Years in the Career of an Aspiring Thug," *Santa Monica Review:* "Testimony" and "The Story of Modern Civilization," *Tikkun: A Bimonthly Jewish Critique of Politics, Culture, and Society:* "At the Capital" and "I Was Very Prolific," and *Volt:* "Planted Document." "50 Years in the Career of an Aspiring Thug," "I Was Very Prolific," and "Closure Opening Its Trap" also appear in *American Poetry: the Next Generation* (Carnegie Mellon, 2000).

This book would not have been possible without the support of my friends, teachers, and family; and without the fellowships I received from the Fine Arts Work Center, the Villa Montalvo Artist Residency Program, and the University of Michigan. In particular, I wish to thank the following people who read various drafts of the manuscript: Lee Briccetti, Gillian Conoley, Elaine Equi, Darcy Frey, Alice Fulton, Christine Hume, Lawrence Joseph, Michele Kotler, Carol Muske, Eileen Myles, Claudia Rankine, Lisa Sewell, and most especially, Sarah Blake and Josh Weiner. Sarah Messer, who helped in countless ways with the making of this book, is singled out for an extra-special thank you.

I'd also like to express my gratitude to Francis Lewis for proofreading, to Walter Smith for his photographic talents and to Austin Thomas for artistic consultation.

Alice James Books gratefully acknowledges support from the University of Maine at Farmington and the National Endowment for the Arts.

Contents

IV.

V.

Whereas the indicative is the mood of fact or of certainty, the subjunctive expresses uncertainty, doubt, or desire, or it admits that something is contrary to fact.

The subjunctive is also used in indirect discourse. It implies that the speaker assumes no responsibility for the truth of the quotation.

—Uland E. Fehlau, *Fundamental German*, Harper & Brothers Publishers, New York and London, 1947.

The subjunctive is evidently passing out of use, and there is good reason to suppose that it will soon become obsolete altogether.

—G.P. Marsh, 1860.

Highway to English

No one would come this way for consolation.
It is a finished and unfinished excursion.

The stone horses are still drowning in the fountain.
The stuffed horses are still prancing at the ramparts.

Everything roadside pretends it is accidental.
Everything that has survived is in rehearsal.

Just look at the painstaking imitations of violation
overcome, including windowpanes broken and mended

in a self-important manner. Even the most ordinary
office buildings have assumed the severity of palaces.

On this trip, it is already too late: there's no avoiding
the highway ahead, a one-way highway in a country

of like-minded highways. There's nothing else to do
but accelerate: past The Museum of the Eating Utensil,

past The Museum of the Round Corner,
past The Chocolate Museum with its reproduction of a battlefield
    melting in the window.

At the cemetery, you pull over and park.
Finally, you can abandon your battered roadster.

Finally, you can run wildly past the unfamiliar
names, the unmarked graves and across the rotting

railroad tracks, smashing your fluttering hands on metal Stop signs
in streets that grow increasingly narrow.

You must turn sideways to squeeze into that empty lot
at the end of town. This is where you were born.

The house with gingerbread trim is now a pile of stones
leading to the mouth of a stove.

You lie down in that mouth and nap.
Inside your head you are inside the house.

You rub your face against the rough stucco walls, lick
the tile floors, run on all fours in search of something sweet.

When you wake, your bed of rocks is drenched
and smoking in the cold.

Red stains the dun sky.
You don't even try.

You curl up and wait for night to come.
You don't wake up.

You only grow more tired.
You only grow old.

Descent

I do it on purpose, despite their warnings: step beyond
the beam into the weak heart of the attic. It gives,

of course, and the fall is slow, granular. I am all tiny bits
showering the parlor, clouding the glow of the chandelier's candles.

My grandfather, oblivious, keeps snoring, one hand gripping
a stick of sausage, the other fondling the leather photo album.

My grandmother, cursing and brandishing a dustpan, scrapes me
off the drapes, flings me in with the kindling.

I hug the Yule log. Coal chunks are my companions.
I accumulate weight, a certain willful smudge.

I grease the floorboards, dent the parquet, press
my face into the planks that fold around my ears.

I am diving headfirst into wood and below
to the deep dank cement of basement.

Here, rubber boots have lined up for a march to the furnace.
Toy soldiers melt, tin guts smeared all over the baseboards.

Two decades' worth of *Life* magazines weep
all over themselves, damp pages lifting and falling
    in the mildewed breeze.

I join in, lying down in the dust, arms and legs X-ing
the entrance to the passageway hidden under the coiled rug.

It leads down to a house of earth, without windows
or doors, one room with roots dripping through the roof.

I imagine being down there:
face down, palms dug in, light shut out,

the ceiling pressing its stomach into my back.
It will be a relief knowing

there's no room
for anyone else, and for myself,

there will be no more
downward place.

50 Years in the Career of an Aspiring Thug

1. Burned Christ to a crisp. 2. On the Betty Crocker burner. 3. Tied a body to the railroad tracks. It wore the clothes of a girl. 4. Later found naked and weeping in the fields. 5. It was a body of straw. 6. It wore a note that said: *I am God.* 7. Drove Father's golf cart into the pond. *My final hole in one,* said the note stuffed in the ninth hole. 8. Stole prize roses from Mother's garden. Wore them on the head, as a wreath, in secret, admiring the Romanesque profile in the bathroom mirror. 9. In the diary: *I will conquer.* 10. Dreamed of making the rank of Eagle Scout. 11. Stole Brother's BB gun. 12. Shot the lights out all over town. 13. Disappeared. 14. Didn't leave a note. 15. Got a job in the city working for the glass company. 16. Checking panes for cracks. 17. Etched curses into every self reflected. 18. Got a job working for the car company, answering the phone. 19. *I'm Henry Ford, on this earth to eat your soul.* 20. Got a job working for the baby food company, counting cans of mashed beets, broccoli, meats. 21. Kept that job. 22. Wrote neat columns. 23. Of numbers. 24. Added with precision. 25. Punched. 26. The. 27. Clock. 28. The. 29. Clock. 30. The. 31. Clock. 32. *One more spot in the spotty night,* scribbled on the forehead in the mirror. 33. Sad brow of the girl on the job in the boss's bed. 34. *I am beads on an abacus.* 35. *Clicked.* 36. *From left to right.* 37. Wore a crown. 38. Of sweat. 39. Bars of the headboard trapped in small hands. 40. Woke as the only one inside the body of mulch, the body of palm smears, the rewired body of blue veins and split hairs, the body of loose and multiplying terms. 41. Breathed zeros in the damp. 42. Monitored ceiling stain's spread. 43. Pondered the unwritten book of the distant. 44. Time card. 45. *That little priest hungry for sins.* 46. Wielded the stolen grease pencil. 47. Blackened the stolen roll of fish-wrapping paper, a record. 48. Of hiding places. 49. *Because street lights got replaced.* 50. *Because fields grew parking lots.*

Signing Up

Painted on the clear body of the pen is a girl
who loses her swimsuit of ink each time she's tipped up.

First Stalin, then Hitler strip her down, her bare toes leaking
signatures across the declaration of war against Poland.

Meanwhile, across the ocean, in America, a textile importer
attends to accounts—the costs of swimsuit material and lace.

All the rage in Germany, he explains, setting his father's gift
down on the horizon of his desk so that the painted girl
reclines, swimsuit intact.

Then he gets back to business, tips the pen up, loses himself
in the draining out. His wife frowns at the nude girl

dancing down the margin, turns to dust the porcelain Christ child
riding a donkey, the porcelain dog balanced on a gold ball.

So this is what is meant by occupied, she would say
later that day, after the emergency ride in the Studebaker,

after coming out of the twilight sleep—
tiny hands in train windows waving good-bye—

after gloves remove the inside: baby girl
blindly grabbing for the deepest sounds.

ah	bay	tsay	day	ay	eff
gay	hah	ee	yot	kah	ell
emm	enn	oh	pay	koo	air
ess	tay	oo	fow	vay	iks
ipsilon	tset				

Was heisst Rechtfertigung?
Bewältigung der Vergangenheit.

1. JUSTIFICATION QUESTIONS

Was the hearse wrought for governing?
Was he hissing, that rector for the gone?
Was his right to finger good?
Was he stricken by time's gun?
Was his story wracked fear to go?
Was history just a flirty theme song?
Was he in she erecting fires to groom?
Was he a she rescued from God's nag?
Was her hope what wrecked that furtive God?

2. INSTRUCTIONS FOR CONFRONTING AND OVERCOMING THE PAST

Bore under verb's ache and hit.
Bow all together for verse gagging her.
Beware the gone-down virility nagging height.
Be waltzing girls, dare to veer, gang and hide.
Be welted damage, a vague, anguished heart.
Be wailing time's lung, a door ventilating hate.
Be witched guns, don versions and hurt.
Be Beowolf, gone, driveling on high.
Be Walt, lost uncle, the verifier, angling hard.

A Girl's Life: in the Photo Album

tiny black triangles, meant for corners of action shots, hover

"the doll's tea party"

"the smile that would not end"

"a funny story"

Learning German

A.

Two dictionaries spread open on the bed,
the girl wakes with her head on *fire,* her pelvis on *überall.*

A sprinkle of red lights rips free of sky and never lands.
Independence Day. The War is over. She will never earn

a Purple Heart. To compensate, her father buys her a dress,
gun-metal gray. Her cousin was once a Brownshirt, then a pilot,

now dead. To compensate, her father sends cocoa, brown soap
and tobacco to someone in Germany. Her fingers travel

the twin rungs of words: She plays at playing
the harp, at writing speeches, at reading her words aloud

to soldiers in formation, to women in aprons leaning out
of windows above narrow, cobblestoned streets. Below

the gray silk, sweat beads up around the scapular, wool bib
adorned by the iron-on face of Christ—gold eyes

aimed at the inside of her dress. Beneath the freckled skin,
the heart slogs out an extra gush—Heart Murmur, sloughed-off

talk between two beats. She keeps time, scanning lines
of definitions, muttering her own invented pronunciations.

B.

She no longer remembers the language her mother says fell out of her mouth as easily as English. She no longer remembers when it was forbidden to speak aloud, in public, what she no longer remembers. She no longer remembers what she no longer remembers being the secret her father was the keeper of. She no longer remembers her father pretending he no longer remembers what she no longer remembers. She no longer remembers her mother beginning to no longer remember the language that was once one of several shifting positions inside her.

C.

She forms sentences beginning with Seldom, Never, and In Vain.
She would be a star pupil except for the handwriting

looping too far above and below the blue lines, ground too hard
into the white page until the words are too dark and deep
       to revise.

She rubs at the ends of sentences with the pink end
of the pencil, lets the paper thin until it opens up.

Like her heroine, Merry Lips, girl-spy who disguised herself
as a boy to steal secrets for the King   (*If only I were King* ...),

she is the one sent out to test the ice on Lake Success.
                                        (*If this be treason* ...).

In summers, when school is out, her brother hunkers down
with girlie mags in the wood-scrap fort.

She wanders off to sit among the tallest grasses on the bluff.
Today, she thinks, *I am a blackboard someone has wiped clean.*

One day, she thinks, gazing down at the highway,
I am going to speak German fluently,

which would be the equivalent of: One night
there was a terrible storm.

Eines Tages ... Eines Nachts ...

Planted Document

Thy Sad On Arm Longr Than Th Othr.
Thy Sad War Wound. Thy Sad Strtchd

By Wght Of Brfcase Ovr Thrty Yars Tm.
Thy Sad H Workd N Lac Wth Jws

N Th Garmnt Dstrct. Thy Sad Mayb H Was
A Jw. Thy Sad Onc Hs Lttl Grl Playd Naz

N Th Suprmarkt, Goos-Stppng, Hl Htlrng
Untl Th Wf Slappd Hr Hard. Thy Sad Long

Aftr Th War, H'd March Th Nghborhood
Lat At Nght, Warng Hs Old Ar Rad Wardn Hlmt,

And Wpng. Thy Sad Th Day H Dd, Documnts,
Wrttn N A Languag Hs Chldrn Dd Not Know,

Brok Opn and Flw As F Tormntd By A Grat Wnd.
Thy Sad Whn Hs Daughtr Pckd Thm Up, Nk Gushd

All Ovr Hr Hands. Thy Sad Th Words Burst
Nto A Thousand Tny Flams And Sh Dousd Thm

Wth A Fr Xtngushr. Thy Sad Sh Smard Th Words
On Purpos, Usng Hr Fathr's Favort Watrng Can.

Nicht

I have *no* friend.
I don't have *any* friends.
You have a friend, *don't you?*   nicht wahr?
You are Mr. Smith, *aren't you?*   nicht wahr?
I am *not* Mr. Smith.   nicht
I know *nothing.*   nichts
I do*n't* know anything.   nichts
He is *not* here *yet.*   noch nicht
Is he here *yet?*
He is *not* here *anymore.*   nicht mehr
I do *not* have *any more money.*
I do *not* have *a* (single) friend.   nicht einen

Nicht arrives, weaving slightly, heavy-lidded, heaving. Nicht wait-
ed all night for the convoy that never arrived then marched all
night toward the one light strobing the night, the never-ending
night, the night cloaked and clicked shut, the night freshly paved
and glistening.

Nicht matches the night and wears it like a circus tent, like a para-
chute, like an armory. The night is not black as one might assume,
but a smoggy sepia darkening. The night is like a brown paper suit-
case getting damp. Nicht has traveled a long way to find the end
of night, the beginning of Nicht, a place where Nicht and night
can stand apart.

But this is not the end of night, this is just a pause, single bulb swinging above the paper perimeter of skyscrapers. Nicht considers the muse chased over so many miles: small glow rubbed into gloomy air. Nicht toes the edge, nudges the bright, and the round cloud of radiance shudders off in the opposite direction.

Mr. Smith observes through the one-way page. Mr. Smith rose early, ready to praise the new flock of trenches. He had already sharpened his pencils. But, instead of another territory to be translated, here is Nicht, smudging up the foreground. Tin cup dangling from a string attached to the sleeve. Hems flapping. Laces splayed. Tardy, sighs Mr. Smith, who had given up.

Nicht reclines beside the ring of light, pretends it is a camp fire, begins to snore. Meanwhile, Mr. Smith gets down to brass tacks, begins by clearing decks: deletes messages, crosses out days on the calendar, tears out pages in the workbook he does not like. All clear, Mr. Smith hits the switch: blue light washes over the wall-sized page, then the silhouette of speech organs contorting. The volume kicking in is like marbles clacking on a parquet floor. Ricochets lasting a long time.

Mr. Smith sighs, moans, writhes in his chair ... then tries to simmer down. Checks the latest stats on extinct dialects, adds this new one to the addendum. Scribbles notes for the English-Is campaign: Your Passport to a Brighter Economic Future. Always in the Right Place at the Right Time. In Service to the World.

Nicht wakes to the drip-drop of some big faucet softening in the far off. The hum of machinery warming up. Nicht wonders about the birthplace left behind. Was the cottage by the shore actually a carnage at the door? Were the stars flares?

What Nicht does remember: being wedged in among others, never allowed to stand alone. Shunted back and forth across a narrow plank. Misunderstood. Mispronounced. Now I am free, thinks Nicht, struggling up, grabbing the megaphone that has appeared prizelike at the center of the ring of light. Mr. Smith climbs high for a better angle.

But Nicht chokes up. Air too thick, tonsils too big or word too wide. The N of that first word caught, rattling around inside the throat. What escapes is barely audible: a cross between a mew and a sigh, a scratch and a spark.

A bad investment, says Mr. Smith, climbing back down the ladder, flinging his pencil like a dart.

Nicht reclines again, limbs drawn in, head bowed down. Light closing to a halo around the mouth. Nicht coughs, hiccups, coughs. Tune of a razor getting stuck, explains Mr. Smith from the orchestra pit. Inspired, Mr. Smith taps the podium.

A new campaign song is forming. An old ditty hacked up, then sharpened. As for the lyrics, something less strident than before. Something more rhetorical. Mr. Smith raises a fresh pencil with a flourish. The naked bulb brightens, the page going transparent.

I Was Very Prolific

Legislators say they want women to have second thoughts.
   —HEADLINE FROM *The New York Times,* January 28, 1998

I was very prolific in my generating qualities.
I was sprouting here and there.
They said I was developing.
They said my heterosexual adjustment
was quantitatively well above average.

Of course, they said, there is always the possibility
she won't cooperate. But I did my best to acclimate.
I said to them: *Just don't rip my nylons.*
I said to myself: *This is not my self.*

Afterward, no matter how much I gargled
or apologized, I couldn't get that force field
out of my head: it sucked and dragged.
It depleted most of the memory banks,
then installed my functions in the outskirts
of a category called *unknown or other.*
Basically, I was subletting a very unlisted condition.
I signed up for Public Resistance,
for Confessional Help, for Social Insecurity.

At headquarters, the police said:
Welcome to our favorite prefab events.
The doctors said: *Let's make a deal.*
The technicians said: *The Traumatic Image Resource Room*
is now out of order.

After the treatments and a brief dreamy episode
involving armed forces, a parasite shaped like a subway system
built its home in my lungs. No matter how precisely
I cross-referenced, no matter how many official reports
I downloaded, I was still not clear. I was vaporware.
I was the pre-data part of a package deal.

And so I have learned to distrust
the blinking signs, the free-floating quotations.

I have learned that my gender is still a risky situation
marred by sexuality, like those B movies, dominated
by chase scenes and ending in predictable disasters.
And, despite the best of intentions, it is not true
groups of humans behave in an aimless,
non-goal-directed manner. Nor is it true

that being stripped and strapped down,
flown like a flag and projected onto the big screen,
is without reward: just look

at the audience turning its one gigantic head,
from left to right, then back again.

What I Wanted To Know Was Through

the window. I watched my reflection

bleeding out to forest—stone in the face,

pine bough cutting the neck, snow for torso.

The distance wore me like a cold, transparent dress.

I was interference of a negligent nature,

the kind imbedded in a TV's static.

When I figured out my reflection needed light to live,

I hit the switch.

I could be in the dark without my being *out there*.

Nothing seemed

to notice.

Autobiography

1.

I am a king's.
I am afraid I may be
Ilia. I am always aware
of my mother. I am furious
with myself. I am going
to sleep (Suicide Poem).
I am Hermes. I am leading
a quiet life. I am my lover's
and he desires me.

2.

I am New York City. I am of
this world. I am reminded
of this vestment. I am still
bitter about the last place
we stayed. I am too near
to be dreamt of by him. I am
yours. I argue. I came too late
to the hills: they were swept bare.
I can only say I have waited
for you. I can't appease
Ashimbabbar, the moon god An.
I can't break with the Dark One.

3.

I carried statues on the ship.
I catch the movement
of his lips. I come. I come
home from you through the early
light of spring. I come to you with the vertigoes
of the source. I crawl up the couch leg
feeling. I did not know where
you kept your heart.

4.

I died for Beauty—
but was scarce. I don't want to be
a nun. I drag a boat over the ocean.
I felt a Funeral, in my Brain. I find my love
fishing. I first tasted under Apollo's lips.
I flee the city, temples. I had eight birds hatcht
in one nest. I had three friends. I have no
embroidered headband. I hear you've let go.
I heard a Fly buzz—when I died. I heard my love
was going to Yang-chou. I Korinna am here
to sing the courage. I let the incense grow
cold. I live on this depraved and lonely cliff.

5.

I love and fear him. I loved her
softness, her warm human smell.
I make this dirge for you Miss Mary Binning
I miss you. I make this song sadly
about myself. I remember we went to the hospital
that day. I never believed that in my broken
life. I put out the worship plate. I raise the curtains
and go out. I remember you in young peaches like jade.
I sat before my glass one day. I saw no
Way—The Heavens were stitched. I see a man
who is dull. I see bodies in the morning
kneel. I shall lie hidden in a hut.

6.

I, too, dislike it:
there are things that are
important beyond all this.
I took a piece of the rare
cloth of Ch'i. I was the Moor
Maraima. I who cut off
my sorrows. I will carry
my coat and not put on
my belt. I will make
love. I wish to paint
my eyes. I write
to make you
suffer.

Speaking My Mind

My mind is of two pages.
On one is a poem

written in a language I do not know,
and on the other, the translation

I have faked. The language I know lies
down on top of the language I don't.

The layers flap against each other.
I am trying to speak my mind.

But the words turn in their tracks
wanting back in.

It is a stampede of stammering
that sounds like I am begging

backward. I drive a hard bargain, selling
myself short, demanding less and less.

I feel cheap and would like to slap myself
to find out which page is the hologram.

But this is when one page hides
behind its mate, goes mute.

I take advantage of apparent unity to make promises,
such as *I shall hoist the broad beam of I.*

But as soon as the echo breaks,
the pages shimmy in opposite directions.

They float in a parallel formation
like old-fashioned faucets:

one gushing hot, the other icy.
This is when the ranting gets interrupted

by apologies. This is when the broad beam of I
chops itself down, one short half

still planted deep, the other fallen
and rolling in the mud.

This is when the page carrying the poem
written in the language I know

glides off in search of a foreign translator.
While the other page perches on the horizon,

folds its verse into a fist, waits to be pried open.

Wise Comma Suzanne

No sentence here.
Just fragment.
A comma dividing names
like a navel.

This body's upper half is Suzanne,
double-breasted, big-chested.

This voluptuousness is born
in origin. *Suzanne* comes from *lily:*
scaly bulb erupting with tall stems, whorled
leaves, and droopy, bell-shaped flowers.

Suzanne sprouts from the white bank
of the left-hand margin, in mercurial shades
of orange, cream, scarlet, even blue.

Meanwhile, the lower half, the base half,
is Wise, and without limit.

Sage, grave, discerning, learned, pious, judicious,
Wise—when attached to female—
becomes wily and well-versed at magic.

This part is all fortune-teller.

This part is smarty-pants without the pants,
with skirts and stretch marks and other marks, and sex
used like a divining rod. This part leads the charge.

United but divided by a pause, Suzanne
Wise has been interrupted, as is her nature,
as is the nature of the world taking precedence.

But she would rather not be
a complete sentence, completely
sentenced. She prefers to be cut
off from expectation, to be a free
association associating with silence.

She has been stolen from the index
by a renegade grammarian who knows
predicate is extra, an under-thing
that halts the rub of word on word, of word
on sticks and balls and arcs of punctuation: all the slick
friction of meaning's excess.

And so Suzanne Wise is stripped
down to her self and a half
curl that hinges halves together,
subjecthood swiveling around
without its hood.

And she bears that bareness
like a shield.

The Diarist

Writing something down means I won't have to remember it.
I start off with numbers: bills, birthdays, my checking account code.
Then I progress to names: friends, acquaintances, friends
of acquaintances I have never met. My mother's maiden name.
Her first name. My middle name, which is also the first name
of my father's mother. So, of course, I must write down
my father's name: first, last and middle. Then the original name
of my birthplace, since changed, and changed again,
by invading countries, the names of which I also add.
Then I list my secret artistic aims, my vague spiritual beliefs,
my most banal fears. I outline my moral and political doctrine,
listing volunteer work I have done or always thought
I should do. I write faster and faster and my writing begins
to feast upon itself, leaping outward and inward at once,
knitting consonants to vowels, knotting colons and commas,
snarling parentheses and ellipses until I no longer recognize
what I want to forget. But whatever it is, it expands—nestlike,
then forestlike, then jungle-ish, like an alphabet garden
gone mad, not from neglect but from excessive
and illegitimate planting. It is a strange comfort;
it is like a brocade pillow sporting a pattern of inkblots
or a flower bed of bedsprings overgrowing a field
of mattresses or a field of mattresses unstuffing themselves—
innards breaking through seams, bloated with fungal life.
And I keep writing as a kind of lying down, as a form
of passing out. To write is to recline is to pull
the slick and flapping loops of script over my head
and watch the white wane, a cursive dawn
splashing all over page after page after page.

Lunchtime in the Kingdom of the Subjunctive

A spoon propels itself out of its soup
as a bone sprung free of skin

or a tuning fork
trembling into the background,

then arcing and returning
as a boomerang.

Meanwhile, the glass of milk glides up and out
of your hand, quietly streaking a gloss

of stars through your suddenly glowing hair.
Meanwhile, toast combusts in a golden dust.

Butter drops form clouds that release an ochre rain.
You grow misty-eyed, nostalgic.

This feeling is alleviated by a sense of dread
and instability as the tabletop turns metallic,

tips and revolves as a chain-saw blade
slicing the floor into windows

you slowly and gracefully crash through.
Splintered glass sequins your skin.

Your hands reaching for the doorknob
sharpen to cones. The door soars.

Your legs run too fast, lose their feet
to curls of smoke drifting up the stairs.

You spend hours, or possibly years, floating around like this—
light-headed, fuzzy-brained,

cotton-mouthed. You have fallen in love
with the way light refracts in impossible ways.

Later darkness barges in horizontally,
like a lawn cutting itself down.

It is night without shadows
and everything is way too shallow.

You are too close to the picture
to see if you're included.

You fall headfirst down the drain
sucking the bright out of colors.

You become somber, colder, a kind of high-quality vinyl,
and, in some places, an old damp velvet.

Meanwhile your head continues to plummet,
has become a potholed highway

splitting into stalks, going to seed
as you talk yourself into the distance.

You are telling yourself: *Do not be afraid.*
You are begging: *God help me.*

You are whining: *If only*
I had not come home for lunch today.

If only I had some kind of anchor
in here. If only I could disappear.

You know you should be ashamed.
This is the kind of compulsive behavior

you are always being criticized for.
But it's not you anymore.

It's that soup bowl,
now soupless and spinning, hovering

and singing, sparkling like a god and spitting
its empty refrain in the faces of all your best selves:

If only _____, *then* _____.
If only _____, *then* _____.

IV

At the Capital

Here, everything is cheaper.
Here, everything is, in fact, being given away for free.

Still, store windows get smashed.
But what's looted are nuts and bolts, planks and posts,
not the dusty appliances, not the polyester outfits.

The plan, according to the alternative press, is to build an ark
or some other form of escape vehicle.

Meanwhile, at the Cafe Cherche Midi, the drunks watch TV:
a rerun of last week's terrorist shooting. They cheer
for the victim who, as he dies, fights the small crowd
trying to hold him up.

Meanwhile, unemployed teachers stand in the rain
at the harbor, waiting for drugs to arrive.

Meanwhile, the town philosopher rides by on his unicycle
crying: *Go home, all of you. Go home.*

But the sidewalks are empty. No tourists come here anymore.

The few that wander in by accident, clutching the outdated
guidebook, search for the statue of the king—the one
with the bulge below the belt, a monument to excessive virility.

But the stony king was struck down years ago
and broken into pebbles by the city's girls,
no longer allowed to be virgins past the age of ten.

So the occasional tourists end up looking for historic graves.

Instead, they find gangs of boys stomping plastic bouquets,
kicking down headstones, writing the names of the dead
on each other's skin with tacks and sticks, with broken glass
and bricks.

Knives and razor blades, once the obvious choice
of children, have been sold out for an entire generation.

The mothers and grandmothers try to keep up appearances.
They scrub the mural depicting smiling, well-scrubbed workers.
They water the small grove of petrified trees.
They sweep the dirt streets.

The plane passing overhead, of course, does not land.
The runway is now a flaming landfill.
The pilot is saying to the passengers:

Below you, please note a diorama of the former capital.
It has been reconstructed as it appeared after the fatal bombing.
We shall be arriving at the new and improved capital
in just a few moments.

The Ghetto of Blasphemy

We stride east across the avenues,
past The Cooler and The Vault, past Hell and Void,
past men dressed as women, women dressed as men, women
dressed as women for work as prostitutes. We are undercover
girls, dressed in big coats, big boots. Underneath, we are
without shirts and full of liquor, looking for trouble to look at:
we have our cameras, we are good students, we are detectives
uncovering ourselves on the piers with the boys
and the men and the hermaphrodites.

We use the warped hood of a wrecked car,
a banister, a flagpole, a fire hydrant, as props, as extensions:
We become humpbacked, double-bellied, codpieced, pointed.
We are statues with attachments. We are broken letters
lying down as shadows on bedsprings, trash cans,
sidewalks lustrous with broken glass.

We pose for each other on this splinter of pavement,
beyond Alphabet City, beyond the last stop of the subway, beyond
the most eastern avenue, on the rim of the garbage river
with its garbage-laden barges. We are reveling
in the vehement pink of the neon-lit sugar factory,
the sultry amber of the blinking caution signal,
the insistent orange of small flames blossoming in trash heaps.

We are happy in our iridescence, in our painted skins
until searchlights splice in, until we are surrounded by authorities
who wear dark blue suits, who carry briefcases, cell phones,

microphones, press passes. Given our differences, we are forced
to give them a look at the insides of our lapels, our pockets,
our hands, our waistbands, our mouths. We give them alibis,
we give them imaginary sources, we give them fake names,
and after they give us warnings, give us tickets, take our money,
take our numbers and descriptions, after they go off into the blaze
of lights and the canyons of skyscrapers in search of more
evidence, we give our real names to the wet cement,
to the night crew's best work, which we claim
because no one else has, which we claim as our fresh,
our recalcitrant page soon to be stepped on, built upon, driven
over, broken open by exploding steam pipes, and repaved.

Abandoning our curse-embossed handiwork, we stride back
across town to meet the somber gray dawn, now silvering
with nickels and pigeons, with our extravagant hair
growing wild and wiry in the static and the gleam of the world
passing through the eye of the hidden camera,
which is recording our crimes on some strip of film,
a strip that will float amidst a profusion of strips
shifting in the breeze like junk mail, like one-dollar bills,
    like tongues.

The Tea Cart Talks Back, Explodes

I carry myself well, despite my delicate build.
I am only glass, teak and brass hinge yet I bear
rows of crystal, the unforgiving brow of a white
bowl, mason jars of drowned cherries, slivers
of crustless bread laid heavy with sugared butter,
petit fours, tiny cups, tiny silver forks branded
with the double S, a butcher knife, ladyfingers.

I had forgotten how completely the rooms differ.

The other was a vault of burdened shelves,
glowering hooks, a coiled rug, a ready rolling pin,
the old woman pinching piecrust with a vengeance.

This one is ablaze
in white light, in white faces and hands, white
tablecloths and the high sounds of light laughter
and wineglasses touched together in a toast.

They sidle up, scan my uses, murmur
over what they will select or refuse.
No one sees the sharp edges or the spit
the old woman hid in the sweetest dish.
They don't know what simmering means.

Not until my shelves begin to shake
and smoke. Cherries slosh and spill.
My wheels roll out from under me, spin
along the hand-waxed floorboards,
while tea leaves get launched to chandeliers.

I can't help myself. I want nothing
but their corralled devotion, the splintering
of servitude, the unhinged and upended.

Advice

It is time for you to stop trying to be so smart.
It is time to abandon those plans for aqueducts,
canals, sewers. It is time to burn your boats,
to jump into the next free dinghy, to run
yourself aground on foreign land. It is time
to smash every inhibition on the shores of progress,
then loll in the rubble, flinging shards of ship
at gulls as you build empires in the sand
beneath a beach umbrella. Basically,
it is time to stop trying so hard.
Instead, lie back and listen to the waves
smashing shells to bits. Think of it
as a chorus goading you to greater heights
or as wild beasts begging to be caged.
Basically, it is time for you to be heard.
Remember to enunciate. Pay attention
to vowels, the way they seduce
regardless of the words they inhabit.
Recognize how the names of things
slide off their thingness like fried fish
from an oily plate. Smell the fishy fragrance,
injected into the steamy air by the mere
mention of *dinner*. Fondle your imaginary
skillet. How hard and dark and hot it is.
This is just the beginning of your power.
You will find new oceans, you will reside
in a do-or-die mode. This is not necessarily
a problem and thus the ironic, absurdist tone
you have become accustomed to

must also be abandoned. You must be
patient. You must quietly await
your one authentic voice. As Pound said,
quoting Beardsley: Beauty is slow.

For me, on the other hand, it is over,
politically, and as a human being.
I will never talk about myself again.
I will be taciturn, modest.
You will continue to look at me
from the outside and not know
what I have suffered. Still,
it may be difficult to forget
that I have been your leader.
It is this indebtedness
that will define you
as my greatest joy.

More Advice

I want to thank you, whoever you are,
for the lovely portrait. However, I must admit,
I feel as if your writing has been aimed
at one half my face, zooming in, slicing off my brow
and enlarging every pore until my chin appears
as a lace flag—easily confused with a surrender hankie
laced with bullet holes—flying victorious
over arid, conquered land.

And my mouth feels like a tunnel that's been
grenaded. Teeth broken and layered
like a farmer's stone wall. Tongue, a fossil
pressed thin and embedded with sediment.

And lately, when I try to sleep, I see your eyes,
closed and pasted on a forehead above another set
of eyes that are blindfolded. I hear what could be
typing or machine-gunning from beneath my rib cage.
I feel a probing in my lungs and gut, and then I see my organs
as gray ponds pressed against transparent skin.

In dreams, we speak face to face
but your face is a metal grate with a lock for lips.
The keyhole mouths: *I want to know who's watching.*
How small we get before we're gone.
I say: *Paying attention is a way of taking*
attendance. I say, *Knock, Knock.*
But the dreams always stop before the punch line.

To please you, I spend my waking hours
naked and talking in accusatory captions,
such as: *She's fooling herself with that imaginary
camera.* Or: *She deserves to be exposed.*
You seem to need doubt. You seem to doubt
need. You seem to be primarily angry,
disenchanted, anxious to clarify
your position. You may want to vary
the tone a bit. You may want to feel less
obligated to me and my story.

The Story of Modern Civilization

1. THE TOWN

This is the town of migraines and decapitations,
buzzsaws, bloody benches, and gin anesthesia,
soldiers drinking plum brandy from dawn on,
young girls rounded up for somebody's pleasure,
men wrapping their stumps in family linens,
kids and pets lying down on yellow lines,
the psychiatrist who denies the accusation,
the painting of the apocalypse hidden away,
the book of angels no one can read.

2. THE PRIESTESSES

We powder our stretch marks with grave dust.
We rub weeds between our knees.
We say *red lily red lily red.*
We predict wars, plagues, great loves.
We unleash tongues clamoring for prayer.
We open wide, swallowing the names we're called.
We suck bullets for a taste of tomorrow.

3. THE SAVIOR

He pounds a metal stud through his hand,
shaves his head, puts on a pin-striped suit,
shoots a pistol at a passing plane.
He locks himself in a footlocker for three days.
No one can guess where he's gone.
He died. He spoke with God. He spied.
He returns—light-headed, bloody-palmed, smiling.

4. THE GOD

I am the electrified surface of skin you stroke.
I am white space between letters, around the eye.
I am the trigger you can pull and pull.
I am the hole you fill with fresh earth.
I am the names you spit out with the blood.
I am charred earth waiting for new life.

The Meaning of (Life on) Earth

The earth is a planet; the sun attracts it.

You forgot to trim the wing flaps
made out of candle wax and curtains.
You forgot how much you love the drink
that is heat, the drunkenness that is lethargy.
Entranced by the leap and snap of bright fringe,
you drifted into the flapping apron of the sun
without a fight. You had only hoped for proximity
to brilliance, to a masterpiece of light and fire.
Instead, you star in your own tactless drama,
a predictable Icarus, a preoccupied Joan of Arc.
You become the prediction of apocalypse
no one believes in: shutters slamming shut
all across the barricaded city. You streak past,
post-curfew, with no one to see your burnished
breasts, your scarlet lips, or your crackling, bannerlike hair.

The aeroplane fell to (the) earth (not into the sea).

Where you land no one bothers to say the word *forsaken*.
In fact, there are no words left for what has been ripped out,
lives shucked of life. A blankness like whiteness
but less substantial rules the land. As if a plaster mold
had broken up. As if a bleachery had been ignited.
You fall even after you have stopped falling,
after we have pulled you out of your contraption,
propeller still hacking at nothing. You fall inside
the cage of ribs, past the stalled-out heart
we press in on until the dumb muscle flexes
dumbly again. We wrap you in something soft
that hardens. We save you for later.

We filled the hole in the garden with earth.

The soft dirt falls
like shorn hair or moth wings
against your face
looking up at the wing tips
of our shoes. Like skyscrapers,
we have a radiant, monumental aspect
you can only appreciate now
that you must see us from a distance.
Bound up in your best clothes, wrists cuff-linked
and crossed over your quiet heart,
you wait for the oncoming
blow, for the heavier shovelings of soil
that are sure to come. Until then, you admire
the dark drift falling from our fingers, filling in the line
of your lips. The dirt grows thick and sticky,
hardening in the chill air like snow
turning to ice turning to glacier
and you are the expired
landscape soon to surrender
to a great divide.

Where on earth are you?

You aren't on earth anymore.
You're out there, making up the atmosphere.

V

I was not thinking of the future but I wanted it to think of me.

—Beverly Dahlen, from *A Reading 8-10,* Chax Press

Maneuvers

The site had been reached
after weeks. It was empty

except for the description
that lacked color or people.

Certain crimes, unnameable,
had once been rumors.

A whole series of questions
lined up, gave up, forgot.

A gap, due to more pressing
news, opened in the face

of skepticism. An impasse
surrounded by dithering

caved in to the silly
enclave, a busted clavicle

of air abutting the absolute
denial of air. Objection refused

to increase, two or a million,
no more than a matter of time.

The upper hand forced a wide swath
to lie down, spread out. An all-out

pull out pushed for deeper
impotence, rammed a fundamental

divide into separate states. Headlines
ordered lids and pens down for cover.

Confessions checked out, then in,
then escaped for good, translated

as dotted lines, disproportionately
lengthened for logic's new territories.

Thus, the deal was cut
to ribbons, made into a hat,

and ratified. A parade of progress
systematically bound itself

to nonburning treaties, awarded
oblique medallions of oblivion.

Because they had to take credit
for pity, sources borrowed

refugees, returned them to the red
light zone, balanced casualties

for the sum of a defunct map.
Unfortunately, the transcription lost

sleep, was reported to be a yawn.
Outraged, readers found everything

but solace in diddling the O
that hid as countless bones,

nooses and holes in accounts
of banks and other likely stories.

Confession

I had my faults.
I had my so-called desires.
I remained open to temptation.
I argued with my colleagues.
I did not reach 100 percent
in my assignments. But I was no pry
pole, I was subsidiary. I was aspiring
to cog. I wanted to be a gullible
sheep or a rowdy-dowdy shepherdess
or a shamefaced sheepdog.
When I learned what I had to be,
I sat down on my luggage set
and wept. Then I unpacked. I decorated.
I raised the roof. I flew my kite.
I removed all the skulls and thieves.
I told my wise leaders where to sponge.
I was less than resistant. I was more than bold.
I was beyond naked. I was technicolor.
I was a brilliant butcher, an innovative
streetwalker, a saucy sales manager.
I knew a good stogy, a fine lace teddy.
I lived for love. I erred accordingly.
I assumed the world condoned my stunts.
It's clearer today. I was misunderstood;
I was in the know everyone else wanted
out of. Today there are no traces
of erasures, and no qualms, no real
wrongs. I made judgments for the best
and by the standards of the time.

Now that it's over I must beg
for attention. I have been robbed
of the limelight that comes with
responsibility. I can only imagine
how hard it must be for you
to believe me, I mean, to hold
blame. I mean, to be you.

Testimony

Because that heckler was a joke,
(she was no lady), we forced her to behave
like a sheep, beat her, forced her
to enter a hole in front of her house,
ordered her to bend her head,
riddled her. We stitched her good.
She could not move or cry.

Later we paid for what we did.
Her father got 8,000—she had not yet bled.
After the first real customer, the price dropped
to 4,000, then 200 for an hour.
After months of effort, our gynecologists
examined her, proclaimed her barren.
The current ransom is 300 or five jugs of oil.

It is important to be accurate, to measure results,
to learn from mistakes, to continue to do what is right,
correct what is wrong and improve what is imperfect
so as to avoid great losses.

Especially these days, as we pass through
the most unfortunate events, overwhelming our country
and friends as if one had happened upon them
by chance, on some secret errand.

To write down our passionate thoughts
at all is already, in some measure, to command
and have our way with them.

Our inspiration comes out of that dreamy
atmosphere in which men have things
as they will. We regret we were forced
to omit so much.

Closure Opening Its Trap

The pigeons have survived.

Or something that is like pigeons, things small and gray,

                                             things perforating
the horizon until the backdrop of creamy clouds unseams

and black-eyed buildings collapse

down into themselves, bottom levels bombed out and vanishing

                              into the upper parts,
like arms pulled back inside sleeves.

                                       Then the bites or scratches

that might be pigeons turn suicidal

in slow motion, scrolling downward

like a description of rain

that overdoes it, boring

holes in the simulated sand, smashing virtual dunes

into crumbs that are actually   crumbling

credits—illegible, off-white names—

followed by THE END,

block-faced, heavy-handed then   melting

in the sudden downpour, then dispersed

as wet, bready lumps drifting out to sea, where the pigeons,

no, gulls now, aim at what appears to be food.

But the tiny birds, beaks packed with debris, fan out

into flocks of feathery smears,

wake of the erasure paving over the flood, a highway

of nothing that bawls and whimpers,

                                        then coughs, hiccups,
chokes.

This is the theme song—

                    dirge mixing itself up

with canned laughter—

beginning to skip,

to skip,

to skip

The Meaning of Nothing

No particular thing, event, action.

As in, nothing was done
to save the body, to recover
the body, to stop the body.

As in, nothing has occurred
to make the body
change its mind.

A thing of no account or value.

As in, the body cares nothing
for the mind's private problems.
As in, the body is nothing
without its private parts.

No part, quantity or degree.

As in, the mind showed nothing
but dumb love for the body's knowledge.
As in, the body used nothing
of its knowledge to protect itself.

To treat lightly.

    As in, the mind makes nothing
    of hardships endured for the sake
    of the body's helplessness. As in,
    the mind thinks nothing of beating
    the body into submission.

To fail in understanding.

    As in, the mind can make nothing
    of the body's childish joy, and vice versa.

The opposite of something.

    As in, the world was created
    from nothing. As in, the mind
    told the body to open up
    its mouth and say something,
    and there was nothing.

Notes

The title of the first poem in this collection is taken from a series of English grammar books for German students: *The Highway to English* by Dr. Wilhelm Frichs (Hirshchgraben-Verlag, 1963).

"Nicht" begins with a translation exercise borrowed from *Study Guide for German, A Structural Approach* by Walter F. W. Lohnes and F. W. Strothmann, Second Edition (W. W. Norton, 1973).

"Autobiography" consists entirely of lines appropriated from the index of *A Book of Women Poets: From Antiquity to Now*, edited by Aliki and Willis Barnstone (Schocken, 1980). The poem was chosen by Heather McHugh as winner of the *Bellingham Review*'s 49th Parallel Poetry Award.

The phrase *I shall hoist the broad beam of I* in "Speaking My Mind" is paraphrased from Virginia Woolf's *A Room of One's Own*.

The italicized lines in "The Meaning of (Life on) Earth" come from *The Highway to English, III* by Dr. Wilhelm Frichs (Hirshchgraben-Verlag, 1963).

Recent Titles from Alice James Books

ALICE JAMES BOOKS has been publishing exclusively poetry since 1973. One of the few presses in the country that is run collectively, the cooperative selects manuscripts for publication through both regional and national annual competitions. New authors become active members of the cooperative, participating in the editorial decisions of the press. The press, which places emphasis on publishing women poets, was named for Alice James, sister of William and Henry, whose gift for writing was ignored and whose fine journal did not appear in print until after her death.

Design and Typesetting by Lisa Clark
Printing by Thomson-Shore